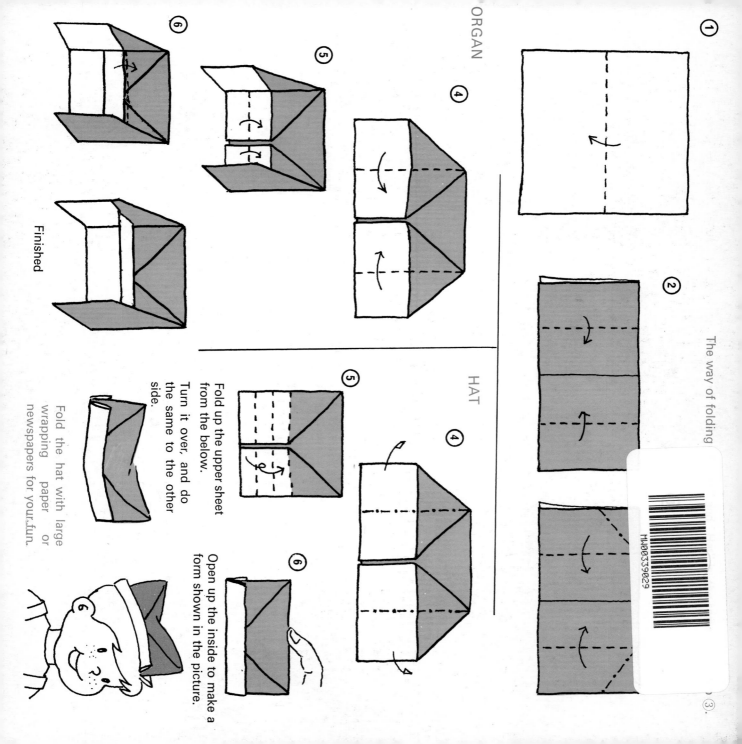

ORGAN

The way of folding

① ② ③

④ ⑤ ⑥

Finished

HAT

④ ⑤ ⑥

Fold up the upper sheet from the below.
Turn it over, and do the same to the other side.

Open up the inside to make a form shown in the picture.

Fold the hat with large wrapping paper or newspapers for your fun.

CICADA

①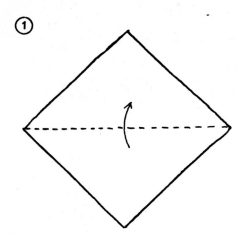

④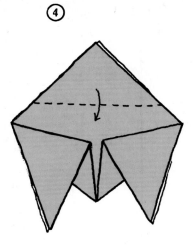

Fold down the upper side
of a sheet first.

⑥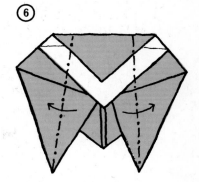

Fold the two corners
forward along the lines.

②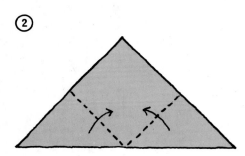

⑤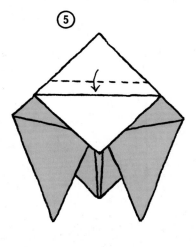

③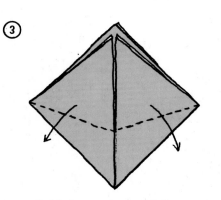

Fold down along the lines.

Fold down the other side
of a sheet along the line.

Finished

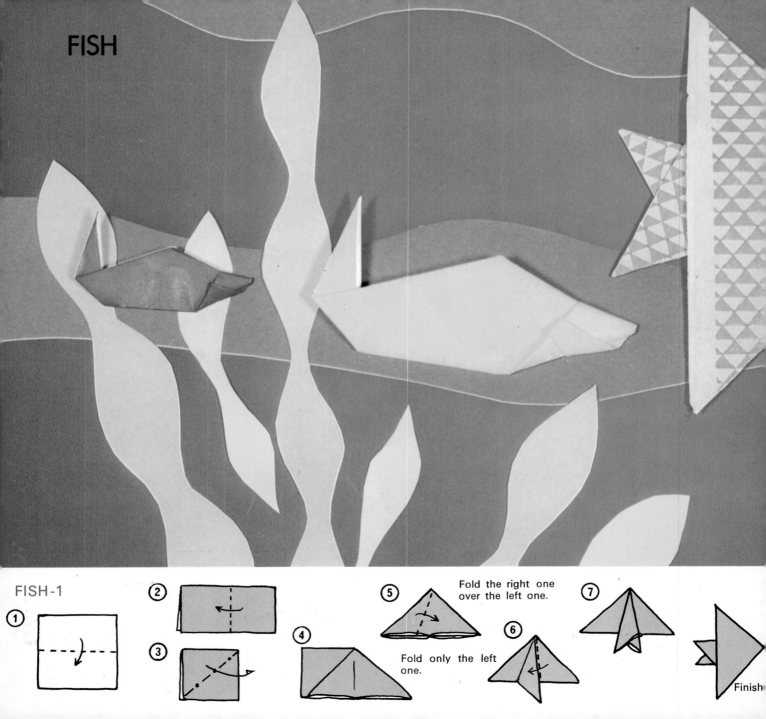

FISH

FISH-1

① ② ③ ④

⑤ Fold the right one over the left one.

Fold only the left one.

⑥ ⑦

Finish

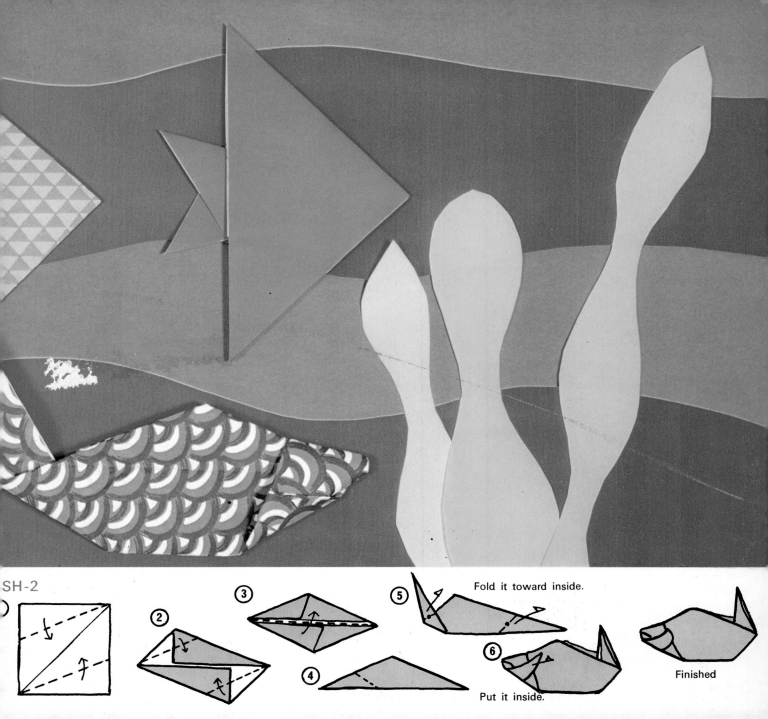

SH-2

① ② ③ ④ ⑤ Fold it toward inside. ⑥ Put it inside. Finished

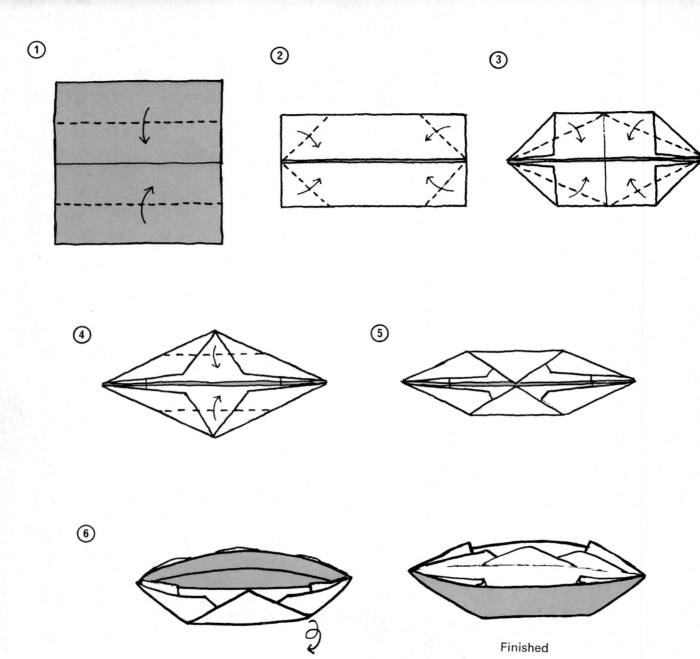

① ② ③

④ ⑤

⑥

Turn it over.

Finished

BOAT

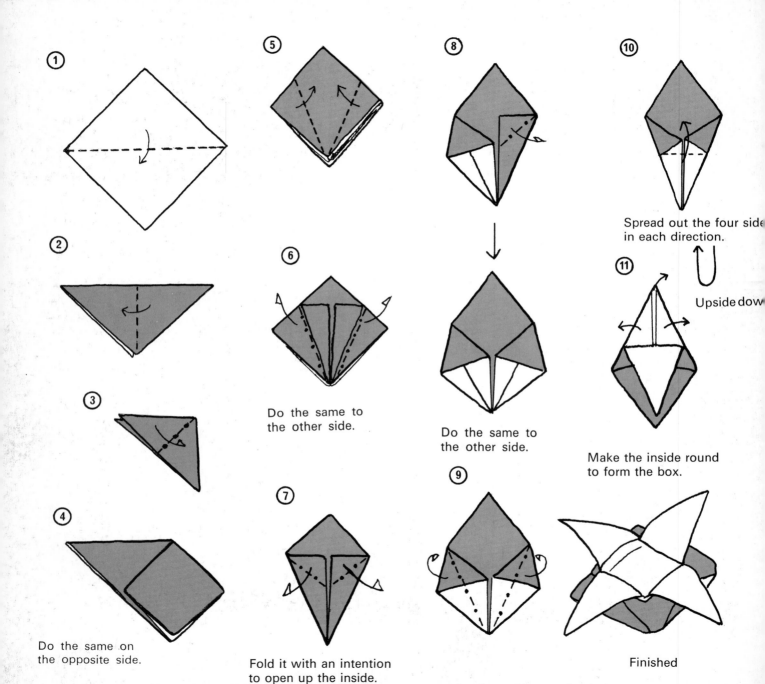

①

②

③

④ Do the same on
the opposite side.

⑤

⑥ Do the same to
the other side.

⑦ Fold it with an intention
to open up the inside.

⑧ Do the same to
the other side.

⑨

⑩ Spread out the four side
in each direction.

⑪ Upside dow

Make the inside round
to form the box.

Finished

JEWEL BOX

PURSE

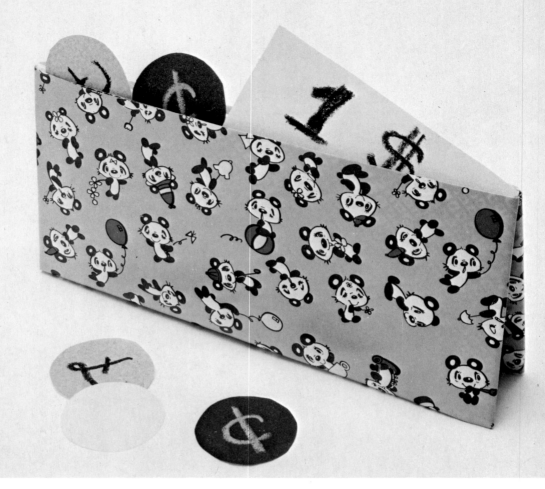

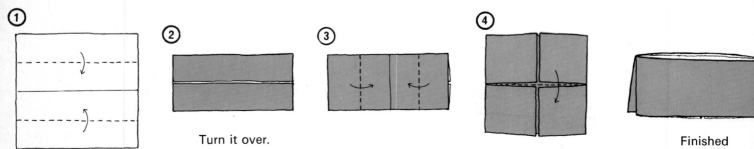

1.

2. Turn it over.

3.

4.

Finished

✳ Basic Rules ✳

—·—·—·— Fold in the reverse direction of the dotted line. This is known as the 'mountain' fold.

– – – – – Fold along the dotted line in the direction of the arrow. This is called the 'valley' fold.

—— Cut

①

②

③

Fold while spreading inside.

④

⑤

Turn it away from you and stand it up.

Finished

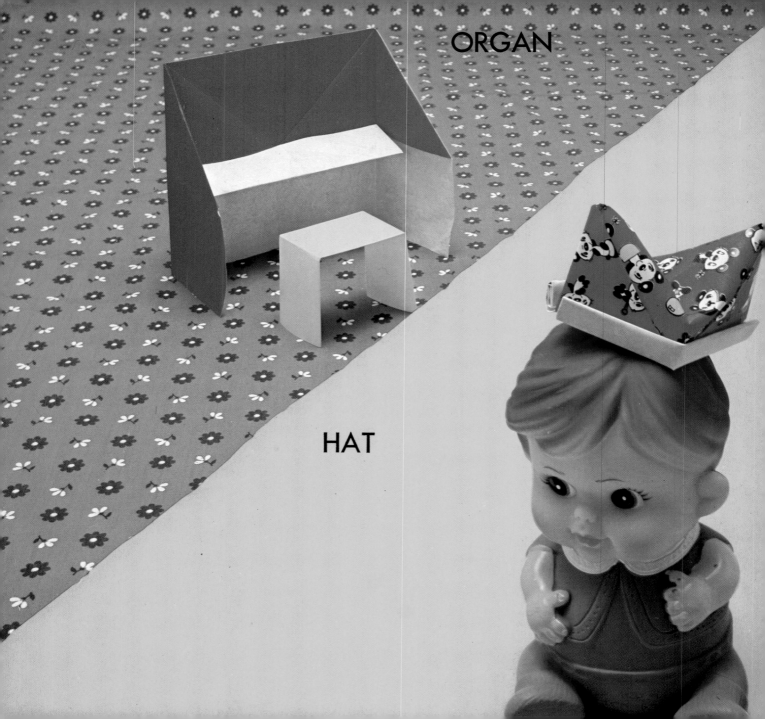

ORGAN

HAT